03587

The Bilingual Education Act:
A Legislative Analysis

The Bilingual Education Act:
A Legislative Analysis

Arnold H. Leibowitz

NATIONAL CLEARINGHOUSE
FOR BILINGUAL EDUCATION

This document is published by InterAmerica Research Associates, Inc., pursuant to contract NIE 400-77-0101 to operate the National Clearinghouse for Bilingual Education. The National Clearinghouse for Bilingual Education is jointly funded by the National Institute of Education and the Office of Bilingual Education and Minority Languages Affairs, U.S. Department of Education. Contractors undertaking such projects under government sponsorship are encouraged to express their judgment freely in professional and technical matters; the views expressed in this publication do not necessarily reflect the views of the sponsoring agencies.

InterAmerica Research Associates, Inc. d/b/a
National Clearinghouse for Bilingual Education
1300 Wilson Boulevard, Suite B2-11
Rosslyn, Virginia 22209
(703) 522-0710/(800) 336-4560

Cover design by Richard Plá, Plá/Mauro Associates, Inc.
Typesetting by Hodges Typographers, Inc.

Library of Congress Catalog Card Number: 80-80121
ISBN: 0-89763-022-x
First printing 1980
Printed in USA

10   9   8   7   6   5   4   3   2

Contents

Contents

Foreword

The Bilingual Education Act: A Legislative Analysis carefully explicates the federal legislation which is the foundation for many bilingual education efforts in the United States today. Arnold Leibowitz begins with a historical look at some of the forces which led to the first act in 1968 and then traces the development of the law through the amendments of 1978. He discusses how the legislation has changed and how Congress has evolved a position on the role of the federal government in bilingual education. In addition to providing extensive notes, the author includes a listing of key legislative documents.

Arnold Leibowitz, a constitutional attorney practicing in Washington, D.C., is vice-president of the Overseas Private Investment Corporation. He was formerly president of the Institute of International Law and Economic Development and legal adviser to the Guam-Virgin Islands constitutional conventions. From 1964 to 1966 he served as general counsel for the Commission on the Status of Puerto Rico. He holds an A.B. degree from Columbia College, a LL.B. degree from Yale Law School, and he did graduate work in jurisprudence at the University of Heidelberg. His publications include *Educational Policy and Political Acceptance: The Imposition of English as the Language of Instruction in American Schools* (Center for Applied Linguistics, 1971) and "English Literacy: Legal Sanction for Discrimination" (*Notre Dame Lawyer*, 1969). In 1979 he prepared a special report for the National Institute of Education entitled "The Official Character of the English Language in the United States."

One of the activities of the National Clearinghouse for Bilingual Education is to publish documents addressing the specific information needs of the bilingual education community. We are proud to add this distinguished publication to our growing list of titles. Subsequent Clearinghouse products will similarly seek to contribute information and knowledge which can assist in the education of minority culture and language groups in the United States.

NATIONAL CLEARINGHOUSE
FOR BILINGUAL EDUCATION

The Bilingual Education Act:
A Legislative Analysis

Introduction

The purpose of this monograph is to provide a clear expo-
sition of the regulatory framework of bilingual education.

This monograph is divided into three sections. The
first sets forth the political background which led to the
passage of the Bilingual Education Act of 1968. The
second is an examination of the existing bilingual education legislation set forth analytically, but with some attention to the evolution from 1968, to 1974, and then 1978. It
singles out the amendments of 1978 so that individuals
familiar with the previous legislation will be able to see
what changes took place as a result of the 1978 congressional action. Others, who may be less familiar with the
previous legislation, will be able to read the section as a
whole for an understanding of the Bilingual Education
Act's provisions as originally passed and as subsequently
amended. The third section addresses the questions raised
by the Congress and recent reports which suggest future
directions and issues for bilingual education. (The key
legislative documents referred to in the text and footnotes
are listed for convenience in the Appendix.)

Historical Background: Tolerance and Restriction

The United States has from the outset been somewhat ambivalent in its English language attitudes. On one hand, the U.S. Constitution makes no mention of language.[1] This is somewhat unusual since the designation of an official language is quite common in constitutional documents, not only in multilingual countries,[2] but also in countries where only one language is generally used.[3] On the other hand, John Jay in the *Federalist Papers* saw the English language as one tie which bound the federal structure. "Providence has been pleased to give this one connected country to one united people—a people descended from the same ancestors, speaking the same language . . . very similar in their manners and customs."[4]

These different points of view throughout our history have been debated with the government choosing to emphasize one or the other as a function of economic needs and political stresses between the established classes and the different visions of America's strength and weaknesses. This chapter will examine a selected few of the many language groups which have emerged and evolved in the United States and will show how their experiences have shaped the federal role in bilingual education.

The Hispanic Population in the Southwest

The Spanish conquistadores came to Mexico in 1519. Many of them intermarried with the Indians, and the mestizo population expanded and gradually moved northward. By 1790 an estimated 23,000 Spanish-speaking people were living in areas which later became the states of Arizona, California, New Mexico, and Texas.[5]

After the Mexican-American War of 1848, Mexico ceded to the United States a vast territory, including California, Arizona, and New Mexico and also approved the prior annexation of Texas. All citizens of Mexico residing within the ceded domain became United States citizens automatically if they did not leave the territory within one year after treaty ratification. Thus, the Spanish-speaking inhabitants of the Southwest became a minority group in a country different in language and culture.[6]

At the end of 1848, there were approximately 15,000 residents in California, half of Mexican descent. But the Gold Rush quickly changed that. Within a year the population expanded to approximately 95,000 people, almost all Anglo-Americans. The Gold Rush not only initiated a monumental increase in the Anglo population but also resulted in a struggle over land, both of which operated to the political detriment of the Spanish-speaking inhabitants.

At the time of statehood, eighteen percent of all education in the state was private and Catholic.[7] These private schools were composed of pupils mainly of Spanish-speaking descent, and the children were taught in the Spanish language under the direction of the *padres*. Initially, these schools were state-supported.

In 1870 California passed a law requiring that "all schools shall be taught in the English language."[8] This linguistic purism in the state-supported school system went hand in hand with the nativistic sentiments expressed in other fields. For example, in the early 1850s California passed statutes suspending publication of the state laws in Spanish, requiring court proceedings to be in English, and imposing a new tax of five dollars a month for foreign miners and a head tax to discourage the immigration of people ineligible for citizenship.[9]

The two earliest New Mexico school laws, those of 1863 and 1869, contained no language provisions. The conditions in the territory leave no doubt that the public schools provided for in the laws had a predominantly Spanish character. There were practically no Anglos in the state; the laws were in fact first drafted in Spanish and translated only later into English. According to the 1874 annual report of the territorial school authorities, the composition of the New Mexico public schools was five percent English speakers, sixty-nine percent Spanish speakers, and twenty-six percent bilingual.[10]

Gradually, Anglo-Americans from the East who were unsympathetic toward Mexican culture came to dominate the territory.[11] In 1891 a New Mexico statute was passed requiring all schools in New Mexico to teach in English[12] as part of a broader struggle over land which was developing between the Anglo settlers and the Mexican Americans.[13]

In Indian affairs, the evolution was similar. Congress made its first provisions for the expenditure of funds not to exceed $15,000 per year to promote "civilization among the aborigines" in 1802; and in 1819 Congress enacted a provision which "still stands as the legal basis for most of the education work of the Indian Service":[14]

The American Indian

> The President may . . . employ capable persons . . . for teaching [Indian] children in reading, writing, arithmetic . . . for the purpose of . . . introducing among them the habits and art of civilization.[15]

No specific mention is made regarding the use of the English language in either the 1802 or 1819 provisions. Both attempt to promote "civilization." That the English language is the "civilized" tongue and the Indian language "barbaric" is implied in these provisions, but not stated.[16]

However, some Indian-initiated educational programs were quite significant. Thus, by 1852 the Cherokee Indian tribe ran a school system of twenty-one schools and two academies—1,100 pupils. Other tribes—the Choctaws, Creeks, and Seminoles, for example—also had begun to establish and operate their own schools.[17]

As America expanded, the desire for the land owned and occupied by the Indians became very great. Initially the hope was that the problem would solve itself: that as the Indians became "civilized" their need for land would naturally decrease.[18] Educational policy was seen as a means to "civilize" the Indians and, thus, permit the taking of their land. President Monroe, writing in 1817, stated: "The hunter or savage state requires a greater extent of territory to sustain it than is compatible with the progress and just claim of civilized life . . . and must yield to it."[19]

The discovery of gold on the Pacific Coast and in the Rocky Mountains had an explosive effect on the population. The promoters of the transcontinental railroads sought grants of land along their routes increasing the pressure on Indian land and tribal units.[20]

In response to the demand for more land, the Homestead Act was passed in 1862, which opened up the plains to white settlers. To facilitate the process, "encouragement was given to the slaughter of big buffalo herds, the Indians' principal source of food. With their meat gone, it was believed the tribes would be forced onto the reservations by the promise of rations."[21]

English language in the Indian schools was first mentioned in the report of the Indian Peace Commission, a body appointed under an act of Congress in 1867 to make recommendations for the permanent removal of the causes of Indian hostility. Its report of 1868, motivated by a combination of humanitarianism, militarism, and expansionism, states:

> . . . in the difference of language today lies two-thirds of our trouble. Schools should be established which children should be required to attend; their barbarous dialects would be blotted out and the English language substituted.[22]

After the treaty period came to an end in 1871, government schools conducted exclusively in English began to be established, gradually displacing the mission schools and their bilingual approach; many of the Indian schools which the tribes had begun to establish and run themselves were also eliminated.

The Experience of the European Immigrant

During the middle decades of the nineteenth century, there was an extraordinary increase in immigration to the United States. It began soon after the Napoleonic Wars in Europe, gained momentum steadily in the thirties and forties, and reached its crest in 1854. Federal statistics (comprehensively collected for the first time in 1820) document the change. In the decade of the twenties, the number of arrivals was 151,000; in the 1830s a fourfold increase to 500,000; in the 1840s, 1,713,000; and in the decade of the fifties, 2,314,000.

In this pre-Civil War period the only large number of non-English speaking immigrants were the 1.5 million Germans who aroused little hostility. They settled in the relatively unpopulated frontier areas of the country where they were unnoticed and generally were in the majority, giving them a political and social advantage not available to other groups at that time. In these farming districts, the Germans initially had no teachers at their disposal who were familiar with English, and in any event, there was little need for a command of English during those early settlement years.[23] Thus, most of the earliest school laws made no mention of the language to be employed in the public schools.[24]

The German migrants did not want English to be excluded, but they asked that German be taught as well. In response to the German demand, the Ohio legislature passed a law by which the German language could be taught in the public schools in those districts where a large German population resided;[25] and in 1840 German-English public schools were introduced in Ohio.[26]

In this initial state of tolerance, Pennsylvania, a few years earlier, had gone even further than Ohio. In 1837 a Pennsylvania law was passed permitting German schools—in some, all instruction was to be given in German—to be founded on an equal basis with English ones.[27] In Wisconsin it became the norm that whenever a newly created school district contained a large German population, teachers were hired and the schools were conducted either exclusively in German or in both German and English.[28]

After the Civil War, immigration continued to increase sharply; from 1815 to 1860, five million; 1860-1890, ten million; and from 1890 to 1914, fifteen million. The increase was in large part due to the steamship line which had replaced the sailboat in the transatlantic immigrant trade, reducing the hazards of the journey and broadening the geographic origins from which one could embark.[29] It was this later migration that became an increasing issue in the United States. From 1860 to 1890, as in the prewar years, immigrants came mostly from the British Isles, Germany, and Northern Europe; but in the later period (1890-1914), they came from Southern and Eastern Europe, from the non-English speaking countries of Russia, Austria, Hungary, and Italy.[30] Without money and with English language difficulties, they gravitated toward the cities where pay was somewhat higher and where the population density reflected the close contact of village life at home.

As the end of the nineteenth century approached, nineteen of America's largest cities consisted of over half immigrants and their children. While 18.37 percent of all Americans were the children of immigrants in 1890, 86.36 percent of Milwaukee's residents were immigrants and the children of immigrants; 80.12 percent of New York's; 77.79 percent of Chicago's; 56.58 percent of Philadelphia's; 71.04 percent of Brooklyn's; 67.46 percent of St. Louis's; 74.98 percent of Cleveland's; and 77.11 percent of Buffalo's. Their ethnic distinctiveness and religious differences—most were Catholic or Jewish—their concentration, their great visibility, and their initial exercise of political power raised great fears among the American establishment.

Restrictionist sentiment grew, aimed at both limiting immigration and restricting access by the alien to the political and economic institutions in the country. The image of the immigrant as unlettered and easily corrupted focused attention on education and the English language as the unifying and uplifting element. Representative of this view is the characterization of the immigrants by Dorman B. Eaton in his major work, *The Government of Municipalities:*

> What spectacle could be more humiliating to an American patriot . . . than those often presented in grog-shops, low lodging houses, and gambling dens, when party leaders and captains . . . are competing . . . among the degraded and criminal emigrants, as ignorant of our laws and language, perhaps as they were regardless of the laws of the country from which they fled.[31]

Restriction and Tolerance

From 1880-1925 English language requirements expanded rapidly gaining special vigor after World War I. English literacy requirements as a condition of voting and holding office passed in over three-fourths of the states of the Union and limited access to the political arena. Statutes imposing English language tests for various occupations from lawyers to bankers restricted economic access to the American mainstream.[32] These hurdles were paralleled in education: thirty-seven states required English as the language of instruction in the public schools.[33] In 1879 the off-reservation boarding school was established, separating Indian children from their parents and imposing a total ban on Indian language customs and dress.

There were some judicial challenges to English language requirements in the twentieth century with mixed results. A ban on German language instruction was overturned,[34] but English literacy tests as a condition of voting were sustained.[35]

By 1968 when the federal government for the first time, by its passage of the Bilingual Education Act, suggested the permissibility—even the desirability—of instruction in the native language, the political context had substantially changed. By 1960 the civil rights movement, gaining strength after World War II, was at flood tide. The executive and legislative branches had both come out rather strongly for civil rights and focused on the deprivations suffered by various minority groups. In addition to civil rights legislation, the Economic Opportunity Act of 1964[36] and the Elementary and Secondary Education Act of 1965[37] had focused on the poor and made education a matter of national policy and priority for all disadvantaged youth.

The result of this legislation was that the needs of Mexican Americans and Puerto Rican groups gained increasing attention. The wave of ethnic consciousness which accompanied the civil rights movement and social changes in the sixties no longer required Spanish-speaking parents to remain mute or to soften their desire that the Spanish language be given a more meaningful role in their children's education.

The 1960 Census[38] counted the Spanish-surnamed population in the five southwestern states of Arizona, California, Colorado, New Mexico, and Texas, and the figures were indeed significant. The total Spanish-surnamed population had increased more than fifty percent over the 1950 totals: to 3,464,999 from 2,281,710. The 1960 figures from Texas showed that the Spanish-surnamed population was 1,417,810 out of a total population of 9.5 million people, or almost fifteen percent of that total. California had the largest Spanish-surnamed population, 1,426,538—a figure which showed an 87.6 percent increase over 1950.

In the other southwestern states (Arizona, New Mexico, and Colorado), the Spanish-surnamed population was also identified and was, in all cases, approximately ten percent or more.[39] On the East Coast, although not as numerically significant, there was a large number of Puerto Ricans, for whom Spanish was the native tongue; there were over 600,000 Puerto Ricans in New York City in 1960, and by 1966, they represented almost twenty-one percent of the total public school population of that city.[40]

The federal government and the individual states had begun to respond to this increased constituency. For example, in 1965 the federal government established the Interagency Committee on Mexican American Affairs [41] to concern itself with Mexican American issues, and on July 1, 1967, a Mexican Affairs Unit began to function within the United States Office of Education. Within the next few years the Equal Employment Opportunity Commission published its first study of Mexican Americans, *Spanish-Surnamed American Employment in the Southwest;* the U.S. Civil Rights Commission held its first hearings on Mexican Americans and published its first report, *Mexican Americans and the Administration of Justice in the Southwest.* The Congress, in the Voting Rights Act of 1965, suspended English literacy tests as a condition of voting where past performance indicated discriminatory administration of the test [42] and, as a special concession to the educated Puerto Rican voter, banned English literacy tests when the voter had completed the sixth grade in an American school where the language of instruction was *other* than English.[43]

At the local level, the New York City Board of Education in 1958 published its comprehensive *Puerto Rican Study* dealing with the difficulties encountered by these native Spanish-speaking pupils in the New York school system.[44] The Texas Education Agency in 1965 investigated the problems of Spanish-surnamed pupils in the Texas schools, and Colorado published in 1967 a general study of the status of the Spanish-surnamed population in that state.[45]

These studies pointed out that education was in the forefront of the concerns of the Spanish-speaking. The 1960 Census statistics on the educational level of Spanish-surnamed students in the five southwestern states showed that Mexican American children had completed an average of 8.12 years of schooling, four years less than their Anglo counterparts. The high dropout rate that these statistics evidenced caused great concern.

Although the Spanish-speaking were the primary force behind the bilingual education movement, the language issue was present elsewhere as well, most notably in connection with Indian children. Indian policy in 1950 focused upon terminating federal recognition of the Indian tribe, eliminating services and relocating Indians into cities.[46]

In the later years of the Eisenhower administration, the emphasis on termination abated; and when the Kennedy administration entered office, it conveyed to the Indians its desire for reversal of the termination policy. A special task force, appointed to investigate the status of Indian affairs, addressed itself to bilingualism in Indian education but did not provide a very strong case for it.[47] It asked only that the Bureau of Indian Affairs make a special effort to keep abreast of the latest developments in language training and instruction and carry on inservice training programs in conjunction with local universities. Under the federal poverty program, additional monies were provided to the Bureau of Indian Affairs, and special innovation centers were set up to develop new educational methodologies for Indians.

That something new was required was clear. The country's Indian educational policies were reflected in the following statistics. In the 1800s the Cherokees had an educational system which produced a "population 90% literate in its native language and used bilingual materials to such an extent that Oklahoma Cherokees had a higher English literacy level than the white populations of either Texas or Arkansas"; in 1969 "40% of adult Cherokees were functionally illiterate."[48]

The culmination of the new approach was President Lyndon Johnson's Message on Indian Affairs delivered to Congress on March 6, 1968. The statement placed the highest priority on the improvement of education for Indians and the control of Indian schools by Indian school boards. It also stressed language needs and cultural reinforcement.

> These schools will have the finest teachers, familiar with Indian history, culture, and language—feature an enriched curriculum . . . a sound program to teach English as a second language.[49]

Moreover, educational theory had changed. Quite apart from the political developments mentioned, there was an increasing interest in introducing foreign language programs in elementary schools. This activity was assisted by a series of government grants under the National Defense Education Act, passed in 1958 in response to the Russian launching of Sputnik. Title VI and, later, Title XI of that act emphasized the retention and expansion of our foreign language resources, a theme which was to be repeated at the 1967 Bilingual Education Act hearings.

> The most active language maintenance institution in the majority of ethnic communities in the United States is the ethnic group school. Over 2,000 such schools currently function in the United States, of which more than half offer mother tongue instruction even when there are many "non-ethnics" and "other ethnics" among their pupils. On the whole, they succeed in reinforcing or developing moderate comprehension, reading, and speaking facility in their pupils. They are far less successful in implanting retentivist language attitudes which might serve to maintain language facility after their students' programs of study have been completed, approximately at the age of 14. . . . the levels of facility attained usually are sufficient to provide a foundation for cultural bilingualism. This foundation, however, is rarely reinforced after the completion of the study in the ethnic group school.[50]

This renewed interest in foreign languages and foreign language teaching enabled new groups such as ACTFL (American Council on the Teaching of Foreign Languages) and TESOL (Teachers of English to Speakers of Other Languages) to assert themselves in educational circles.

There were increasing numbers of experiments in bilingual programs to meet the needs of particular communities. Dade County in Florida (responding to the educational wishes of the Cuban refugees), Rough Rock School in Arizona (run by an all Navajo school board), and a number of cities in Texas and California initiated programs and experimental approaches testing different methods to reinforce the cultural backgrounds of the community and meet their educational needs.[51] The international field as well provided paradigms and suggestions for action as a number of countries initiated and extended bilingual programs.[52]

The National Education Association (NEA) late in 1966 sponsored a conference on the education of Spanish-speaking children in the schools of the Southwest, which led to the publication of NEA's report entitled *The Invisible Minority, Pero No Vencibles.* This report strongly recommended instruction in Spanish for those children who speak Spanish as a native tongue. In April 1967, at a San Antonio, Texas, conference on the Mexican American, demonstrations were given of the work of bilingual and English-as-a-second-language programs already established in a few elementary schools in Texas. One of the major conclusions of the conference was the need for bilingual education with a call to the federal government to assume an important part of this responsibility.

Need and experience had conjoined for the establishment of a nationwide bilingual education program.

The Terms of the Bilingual Education Act

At present, the act embraces those "of limited English proficiency." Estimates are that there are 3.5 million students with limited English proficiency, only 250,000 of which are served by Title VII.[53]

The 1967 Senate Bill as introduced by Senator Ralph Yarborough directed itself to the Spanish-speaking only: "In recognition of the special educational needs of the large numbers of students in the United States whose mother tongue is Spanish and to whom English is a foreign language."[54]

The approach was rationalized on the basis of their number and different history from that of other groups.

Breadth of Coverage

All Non-English Proficient Students

> We have limited this bill to the Spanish language because there are so many more of them than any other group. If you spread this idea to every language it would fragment and destroy the bill. There is also a basic difference between the Spanish-speaking and the other non-English-speaking groups. If you take the Italians, Polish, French, Germans, Norwegians, or other non-English-speaking groups, they made a definite decision to leave their old life and culture and come here to a new country and set up a way of life here in accordance with ours, and we assumed they were consenting at that time to give up their language, too.
>
> That decision to come here carried with it a willingness to give up their language, everything.
>
> That wasn't true in the Southwest. We went in and took the people over, took over the land and culture. They had our culture superimposed on them. They did not consent to abandon their homeland and to come here and learn anew. They are not only the far more numerous group, but we recognize the fact that they are entitled to special consideration.[55]

The Yarborough bill defined the Spanish-speaking student by birth: "Elementary and secondary school students born in, or one or both of whose parents were born in, Mexico or Puerto Rico, and, in States for which such information is available, other students with Spanish surnames."[56]

Both the limitation to the Spanish-speaking and the definition were sharply attacked by other members of Congress and educators.

> It is most doubtful whether the goals of these measures can be attained if its provisions are limited to one language and one culture alone. Unless all Americans regardless of their national origin are made to feel that the preservation of the various languages and cultures brought here by immigrants is important to the United States, there is little reason to believe that such a program restricted to Spanish alone can be successful.[57]

> The most serious defect of S. 428 is that it recognizes only the problems of the Spanish-speaking population. There are many other groups across the land who have the very same problem who would be ignored by this legislation. There are, for example, French speaking people in Louisiana and the far northeast. There are Indians scattered throughout the country, some on reservations, and others, in fact some twelve thousand or more organized groups in this country with ethnic interests of one kind or another. Each one of these organizations, and the ethnic groups they represent, has a real interest in Federal programs dealing with the special problems of the non-English-speaking citizens of this country. The bill as drawn ignores these interests and denies to these other groups what it gives to the Spanish-speaking. I believe that this is unjust, and may very possibly be unconstitutional. It appears to me that in view of our long history of pluralism, and in view of our continuing efforts to promote mutual respect and tolerance, we would be inviting grave and justly deserved criticism from many ethnic groups if we recognize the problems of only one.

> No matter whether the legislation is aimed at one group, which I believe would be wrong, or whether it intends to assist all non-English-speaking citizens, I believe that the definition of terms should not include a national origins test, and should not be restricted to persons born in a designated foreign country, or whose parents were born in such a country.

> There are many thousands of people in this land who do not speak English even though their families have been here for many generations.[58]

In the House of Representatives at about the same time a number of similar bills advocating bilingual education were introduced, most notably by Congressmen Augustus Hawkins and Edward Roybal of California and Congressman Jerome Scheuer of New York.[59] The Hawkins-Roybal bill expanded on the Yarborough bill to include assistance to the French-speaking as well, and the Scheuer bill authorized bilingual instruction for all children whose native tongues were not English.

The final 1968 law adopted the broader approach and was directed at "children who come from environments where the dominant language is other than English."[60] Both the Spanish language limitation and the definition which linked the Spanish-speaking to national origin were eliminated. This expansion of the program was in keeping with the Johnson administration's position which supported bilingual programs in principle, although it felt much of the need was being met by existing educational activity.

> The primary beneficiaries of any nationwide bilingual education program would undoubtedly be Spanish-speaking children. But there are also other groups of children needing special programs whose home language is not Spanish. There are French-speaking children in Louisiana and near the Canadian border, children of oriental ancestry, and American Indians in significant numbers in various areas.
>
> We expect that the number of children from other linguistic groups will increase in the next few years as a result of last year's liberalization of the Immigration Act.[61]

The 1974 amendments broadened the definition of those included to children of "limited English-speaking ability," and the 1978 amendments changed the law to direct it at individuals with "limited English proficiency."[62] The 1978 law expanded the act's coverage considerably. The change was also made to eliminate the somewhat pejorative connotation of the previous law and to maintain the focus on English learning while allowing administrative flexibility. The new definition no longer requires children to be removed from bilingual programs prematurely (once they have gained the ability to *speak* English although their *overall* English proficiency is limited). On the other hand, students would not continue receiving bilingual instruction after they have developed English proficiency.[63]

This 1978 definition may be contrasted with the suggestions made by the National Council of La Raza which sought to add a bicultural element to the bilingual description and to broaden the scope and objective of the act beyond a mere improvement of English language abilities by extending it to encompass overall cognitive and affective development. The council recommended changing the statutory direction from 1974's "children of limited English-speaking ability'' to "children with linguistically different skills'' and changing the goal from "to achieve competence in the English language'' to providing "opportunities to expand their conceptual and linguistic abilities and potentials in a successful and positive manner, and enhance cultural and ethnic pride and understanding.''[64]

The same thrust was recommended by the National Association for Bilingual Education when it proposed broadening the legislation from an emphasis on improvement and development of English skill to a more comprehensive educational process—which "facilitates the mastery of two or more languages (one of which is English).'' The association recommended changing from "limited English-speaking children'' to "children with linguistically different skills'' and providing eligibility for all children rather than limiting eligibility to children of limited English proficiency.[65]

The 1978 statutory language arose in the Senate embracing some of the ideas which were in the original House bill. In discussing the 1978 amendments, the House Committee broadened the criteria of eligibility to include those "who cannot read, write, or understand English at the level appropriate for their age and grade''; entrance into the program was no longer to be based solely on English speech. Under this broader definition the local school districts would still have the responsibility for making determinations of which individuals would participate in accordance with the other requirements of the act.[66]

Thus, the term "limited English proficiency'' refers to individuals (1) not born in the U.S.; (2) whose native language is other than English; (3) who come from environments where languages other than English are dominant; and (4) "who are American Indian and Alaskan Native students and who come from environments where a language other than English has had a significant impact on their level of English language proficiency'' and, "by reason thereof, have sufficient difficulty speaking, reading, writing, or understanding the English language to deny such individuals the opportunity to learn successfully in classrooms where the language of instruction is English.''[67]

The 1978 definition broadening the act's scope to reach those "of limited English proficiency'' was reinforced by the 1978 Senate Report which noted the desire to expand the existing outreach of the program. The act, therefore, charged the Commissioner in the consideration of applications ''to give priority to . . . geographical areas and . . . to assist children in need that have historically been underserved by programs in bilingual education.''[68] Specifically, it also noted the ''potential need for bilingual education programs among Franco-Americans and Portuguese-Americans in New England and Spanish-speaking persons of Caribbean origin throughout the Northeast,'' and urged ''the office of Bilingual Education to give appropriate attention to applications designed to meet this need.''[69]

Indian Students

The expansion of the legislation beyond the needs of the Spanish-speaking, although related broadly to a number of ethnic groups—the French, Polish, and Chinese were specifically mentioned in the 1968 House hearings—was particularly related to Indian education. Statistics were presented by tribe on achievement, and considerable testimony, both by HEW and the Department of Interior, in addition to Indian groups, focused on the educational needs of Indian children. To some degree, this was linked to additional control being transferred by the federal government to the Indian with respect to curriculum and school staffing.[70] The official executive position was not very supportive; the educational benefits of bilingual education were desirable, but such a program would be difficult to implement.

> If either bill is favorably considered, we urge that it be amended to permit the bilingual assistance program to be extended to children and teachers in elementary and secondary schools operated by this Department for American Indians. We also recommend that it be amended to permit the program to be extended to the Trust Territory of the Pacific Islands.
> The Bureau of Indian Affairs has been aware of the possibilities of bilingual instruction for some time, having developed a few bilingual teaching materials some 25 years ago only to have the movement stopped by the advent of World War II. Since that time such programs have not appeared to be practical due to the difficulty of developing and planning them while at the same time having to operate a full-fledged school system. With the added sophistication that has evolved in the general field of foreign language teaching and learning, it poses an exciting possibility for the Indian children of America who need the dignity and strength such a program could add to their schools and to their intellectual development.[71]

Prior to 1978 the law provided for carrying out programs to serve ''individuals on reservations where the school is approved by the Commissioner.''[72] Under these circumstances, the commissioner could make payments to the Secretary of the Interior to carry out the purposes of the act.[73]

The 1978 amendments changed somewhat the provision of bilingual education for Indian children by providing that the commissioner may fund applicants directly to carry out programs of bilingual education for Indian children on reservations rather than, as in the past, to have to make payments to the Secretary of the Interior to serve these educational needs.[74]

Special Puerto Rico Provision

The 1978 amendments, in addition, made a special provision with respect to children in Puerto Rico. The 1974 Act permitted the Commonwealth of Puerto Rico, like local governments in the continental United States, to improve the English proficiency of children residing in Puerto Rico. But the law now also provides that the Commonwealth of Puerto Rico may serve the needs of students with limited English proficiency *in Spanish*. The amendment is designed to serve those children who return to Puerto Rico from the States who are unable to function adequately in Spanish.[75]

Children in Private Schools

The Bilingual Education Act, from the outset, provided for participation by private schoolchildren in the programs. Nevertheless, participation by this segment of the school population was very small. The 1978 amendments strengthened the commissioner's power to withhold approval of an application or to reallocate funds to assure that children of nonpublic schools are included in the program.[76]

> The Committee adopted this amendment in response to the serious problems of a lack of participation of private school children in bilingual education programs. It is the clear intent of Congress that there be equitable participation of these children in Title VII programs.[77]

General Purposes

The 1968 Bilingual Education Act was directed at ''the special education needs of the large number of children with limited English-speaking ability in the United States.''[78] This broad statement of purpose reflected the Congressional concern for and recognition of the special needs of children coming from homes where the dominant language was other than English. Thus, Senator Ralph Yarborough (Democrat, Texas), who introduced the first bilingual education bill in the Senate,[79] stated in his opening address:

> Our educational policies on the teaching of the Spanish-speaking have not been among our more enlightened areas of educational endeavor. For instance, take our children who speak only Spanish. If there were only a handful, a few hundred, you couldn't afford to establish separate methods of instruction, but millions of children from Spanish-speaking homes come to schools speaking only Spanish.
> The tragic results are shown in the dropout rate. Among adults 25 and over, Mexican-Americans in 1960 had an average of 7.1 years of schooling, as compared to the 12.1 years for Anglos, and nine for non-whites. The gap between Anglos and Mexican-Americans is 5 years, or 41 percent.[80]

The dropout rate was to be repeated again and again throughout the hearings as an indication that matters had gone wrong. But, although there was agreement on the effect on the non-English-speaking child of the present educational system, the reason was unclear.

To some, the issue was psychological.

> Imagine the situation that confronts a certain youngster from my part of the country. A youngster spends his formative years in the warm, friendly environment of his family and friends—an environment in which Spanish is spoken. At the age of 5 or 6 he is taken to school. What a profound shock he encounters the first day there, when he is made to know in no uncertain terms that he may speak no Spanish at school. He must speak English, a language which he scarcely knows, both in the classroom and on the playground. If he is caught speaking Spanish, he will be punished.
> Expert witnesses who will appear later before this subcommittee will comment on the psychological damage which such practices rendered unto millions of children. Even to a layman the injustice and harm of such practices are obvious. Unfortunately, this practice has all too often been the rule rather than the exception in the education of children from Spanish-speaking backgrounds.[81]

This idea of strengthening one's self-image reflected current educational thinking relating one's image of self to both learning and maturity.[82]

> The four-year-old placed in a relaxed atmosphere with an unstructured program learns language effortlessly. Following pursuits which interest him, he has the need, the desire, and the opportunity to communicate in the new language. Our program has stressed the expansion of the child's world. We have been

interested in sensitizing him to the sight and sound and feel of experience and in helping him to differentiate it and develop the vocabulary necessary to describe it.

These children, by virtue of their language training and their broadened experience, are now able to start kindergarten on an equal footing with their peers. They start without the frustration and the experience of failure.

They are accustomed to the sweet feeling of success—and the pattern can continue.

This pattern can be extended. It must be expanded to include not only the economically deprived, but those who are deprived by virtue of their language difficulty.[83]

The educational need was linked also to broader issues of economic opportunity. Bilingual education, a new approach to education, represented the hope that the traditional avenue in American society—education—would open the door to the disadvantaged non-English-speaking group.

There is [sic] still discrimination and inadequate job opportunities for the impoverished, poorly educated Mexican-American. I am convinced that better education is the key that will open the door of equal opportunity to this patient, very worthy ethnic group.[84]

According to a report on poverty just completed at Texas A&M University, families with Spanish surnames are much more likely to be poverty stricken than Anglo-American or Negro families.

The A&M report shows that there is a clear relation between poverty and low education; and the Spanish-Americans are Texas' least educated major group.[85]

Some related the bill to the immigrant tradition in the United States.

Let me conclude in a more general tone. This bill would contribute to increased cultural and social maturity in our society.

Let us show long-range leadership by making it possible to enjoy our cultural diversity. Let us never forget that our great strength has stemmed from being a land of immigrants. Whether Irish, Jew, Scot, Swede, or Mexican, all races and nationalities have [contributed] in years before, and will contribute more to our unique society. As Americans first, cultural diversity simply benefits all of us.[86]

There was a recognition that what was being asked was novel, somewhat different from the approach of other language groups within the United States. Here were groups requesting assistance to maintain their cultural strength and language, but this was necessary to assist their children's self-image and permit the learning process to take place.

> Our children suffer from a poor self-identity because they speak a foreign language. A bilingual educational program can impart knowledge and pride in their ancestral culture and language.[87]

And the historical experience was different. The Spanish-speaking and Indian groups, the key minority language groups to be served by the legislation, had become part of the United States, it was said, by conquest rather than voluntary migration.

The bilingual approach was also supported by some representatives of other language groups. Thus, the General Secretary of the YIVO Institute for Jewish Research testified:

> America has traditionally been a monolingual country. Immigrants have been expected to learn English as quickly as possible and quite frequently were encouraged to abandon their ancestral language and culture with all deliberate speed. The bill, now before the Senate, is important in large measure because it clearly announces to bilingual Americans that not only does the United States Government not expect them to forget their ancestral language and culture, but it is prepared to support their maintenance with funds and other resources.[88]

The multipurpose character of the legislation was reflected in the statute which remained broad and very general on educational purpose and approach.

Declaration of Policy:

> In recognition of the special educational needs of the large numbers of children of limited English-speaking ability in the United States, Congress hereby declares it to be the policy of the United States to provide financial assistance to local educational agencies to develop and carry out *new and imaginative elementary and secondary school programs* designed to meet these special educational needs. (emphasis supplied)[89]

The committee reports made clear that the broad, unspecific charges were purposeful.

> The purpose of this new title is to provide a solution to the problems of those children who are educationally disadvantaged because of their inability to speak English.
> The solution to this problem lies in the ability of our local educational agencies with high concentrations of children of lim-

ited English-speaking ability to develop and operate bilingual programs of instruction.[90]

Because of the need for extensive research, pilot projects and demonstrations, the proposed legislation does not intend to prescribe the types of programs or projects that are needed. Such matters are left to the discretion and judgment of the local school districts to encourage both varied approaches to the problem and also special solutions for a particular problem of a given school. The legislation enumerates types of programs as being illustrative of possible solutions.[91]

Specific Purposes

Bilingual education was to accomplish three purposes: (1) increase English language skills, (2) maintain and perhaps increase mother tongue skills, and (3) support the cultural heritage of the student.

The threefold purpose and the interrelationship was set forth by the Puerto Rican Resident Commissioner in his testimony urging the passage of the Bilingual Education Act of 1968.

The solution, however, is not so easy, for at the same time we must produce fluency in the English language. I wish to stress that I realize the importance of learning English by Puerto Ricans and other minority groups living in the States. I concur fully in Senator Yarborough's statement that "it is essential in a pluralistic land such as ours that we have a common language and means of communication in order to live and work together." But I do not feel that our educational abilities are so limited and our educational vision so shortsighted that we must teach one language at the expense of another, that we must sacrifice the academic potential of thousands of youngsters in order to promote the learning of English, that we must jettison and reject ways of life that are not our own.

The essence of my legislative proposal is simple in concept and structure: I propose the establishment of programs which (a) will utilize two languages, English and the non-English mother tongue, in the teaching of the various school subjects, (b) will concentrate on teaching *both* English and the non-English mother tongue, and (c) will endeavor to preserve and enrich the culture and heritage of the non-English-speaking student.[92]

The multipurpose role of bilingual education was reiterated during the passage of the 1974 Bilingual Education Amendments.

. . . bilingual education involves the use of two languages, one of which is English, as mediums of instruction to assist children of limited English-speaking ability. Both languages are used for the same student population—not as an isolated effort, but as a key component of a program embracing the total curriculum.

Rather than an objective in itself, bilingual education is part of a much larger goal: encouraging a child of limited English-speaking ability to develop fully his individual skills and talents. It is the use of the child's native language and respect for his cultural background that best distinguished bilingual education from programs more narrowly focused, such as ESL and remedial reading.[93]

The act tread carefully between the issues of language maintenance v. transition, cultural pluralism v. utilization of the mother tongue solely to assist in learning English. The manual for project applicants and grantees which was issued by HEW shortly after the act's passage reaffirmed both approaches.

It is intended that children participating in this program will develop greater competence in English, become more proficient in their dominant language, and profit from increased educational opportunity. Though the Title VII, ESEA program affirms the primary importance of English, it also recognizes that the use of the children's mother tongue in school can have a beneficial effect upon their education. Instructional use of the mother tongue can help to prevent retardation in school performance until sufficient command of English is attained. Moreover, the development of literacy in the mother tongue as well as in English should result in more broadly educated adults.[94]

To Increase English Language Skills

Increasingly, Congress has emphasized the English language purpose. Thus, in passing the 1974 law, Congress stated:

The goal of the program in the Committee bill is to permit a limited English-speaking child to develop the proficiency in English that permits the child to learn as effectively in English as in the child's native language—a vital requirement to compete effectively in society.[95]

The primary importance of English is underscored also in the 1978 declaration of policy which is to "demonstrate effective ways of providing for children of limited English proficiency, instruction designed to enable them, while using their native language to achieve competence in the English language."[96] The 1978 law requires the commissioner to develop models to evaluate bilingual education programs to determine the "progress made by participants therein attaining English language skills."[97] This latter requirement and the changed definition of the population to be served assured a response to the American Institutes for Research's evaluation study which found that Title VII students were doing no better than non-Title VII students in English learning.

> In general, across grades, when total Title VII and Non-Title VII comparisons were made, the Title VII students in the Study were performing in English worse than the Non-Title VII students. In Mathematics, across grades, they were performing at about the same level as Non-Title VII students.
>
> Generally, less than a third of the students in the Title VII classrooms were there because of their need for English instruction (limited proficiency in English) as judged by the classroom teacher.
>
> As part of the data collection efforts, each project director was asked, "After the Spanish-dominant child is able to function in school in English, what happens to the child?" Eighty-six percent reported that the student remains in the bilingual project.
>
> These findings reflect Title VII project activities which run counter to the "transition" approach strongly implied by the ESEA Title VII legislation. (Transition in this sense implies that the native language of the student with limited English-speaking ability is used temporarily as a bridge to help the student gain competence in English. Under this approach, when a student is able to function in a regular English instruction classroom, he or she is transferred out of the bilingual project classroom.) In fact, project goals were more consistent with a maintenance approach to bilingual education.[98]

The changed definition of the population to be served to those of limited English proficiency also reflected in part the concern of the Congress that a segregated minority group was being created. A number of witnesses noted this during the hearings.

> There is nothing in the research to suggest that children can effectively learn English without continuous interaction with children who are native English speakers, yet the Federal money has supported programs with only about one-tenth Anglos in the average class. In a society where Spanish-surname children are now more segregated than blacks, according to some measures, and where the Supreme Court has found such segregation unconstitutional, a program that tends to increase separation, raises very serious questions. In a number of cities, officials in bilingual programs have attacked desegration orders and asked that Hispanic schools be exempted for educational reasons.
>
> When the bilingual education title is revised I would strongly recommend that Congress require integrated bilingual student bodies wherever possible.[99]
>
> Another reality that we are facing is the effect that desegregation plans are having on bilingual education. We believe that the issue is not so much a conflict in goals as it is the need for resources to expand the program in order to provide more multicultural settings for bilingual education.[100]

The 1978 law addressed the issue in two ways: by aiming the program at children with limited English language proficiency, it permitted flexibility of classroom placement. In addition, it specifically provided for up to forty percent English-speaking students in the classrooms.

> In order to prevent the segregation of children on the basis of national origin in programs assisted under this title, and in order to broaden the understanding of children about languages and cultural heritages other than their own, a program of bilingual instruction may include the participation of children whose language is English, but in no event shall the percentage of such children exceed 40 per centum. The objective of the program shall be to assist children of limited English proficiency to improve their English language skills and the participation of other children in the program must be for the principal purpose of contributing to the achievement of that objective.[101]

The Senate committee elaborated on the requirement:

> The issue of the extent to which English-speaking children should be permitted in Title VII projects was addressed by the Committee in the following manner. The bill allows the participation of English-speaking children but adds that they shall not exceed 40 percent. It was felt that the presence of English-speaking children would provide peer models for children with limited English proficiency. This is an important aspect of these children learning English. It was also felt that the presence of English speakers would reduce the segregation of children with limited English proficiency and provide positive experiences for English speakers by exposing them to other languages and cultures. The 40 percent maximum allows a wide range of flexibility for adaptation to local situations.[102]

To Maintain and Increase Mother Tongue Skills

The other goals of bilingual education, use of the native tongue and support for the cultural heritage of the minority language student, were retained in the 1978 law, but were specifically subordinated to the English language emphasis. Thus, bilingual education is defined as a program designed for children with limited English language skills in which there is "instruction . . . in English and, *to the extent necessary to allow a child to achieve competence in the English language,* the native language of the children of limited English proficiency. . . ." (emphasis supplied)[103]

The House Report attempted to deal with the transition v. maintenance argument by its reaffirmation of the native language role:

Since the inception of the Act, debate has raged unresolved over the extent to which native languages should be taught and at what stage students are ready to move out of the bilingual program.

Controversies over so-called maintenance or transitional approaches tend to confuse the issue, since these terms mean different things to different people and since there is general agreement that some instruction in the native language is necessary to help students strengthen language skills and develop in other academic subjects.[104]

The House also saw the broadened outreach as supportive of native language maintenance.

The Committee bill deals, to a certain degree, with this issue by broadening the definition of children who can participate in programs to include those with an adequate English-speaking ability but who have difficulty reading, writing or understanding English. Under this broadened definition, though, the local school district would still have the responsibility for making determinations of which individuals would participate in accordance with the other requirements of the Act.[105]

The 1976 General Accounting Office (GAO) report, which examined the bilingual educational program, had found as one of the factors adversely affecting academic achievement of limited English-speaking children, the fact that "the dominant language of the limited English-speaking children might not have been used enough for classroom instruction."[106] The 1978 legislation did not follow up on this comment.

To Support the Child's Cultural Heritage

Although Congress did not adopt the specific mention of *bicultural* along with *bilingual* as suggested by the U.S. Commission on Civil Rights[107] in 1975 and the National Council of La Raza[108] in 1977, it continued its support of the cultural heritage goal in the 1978 law.

The 1974 law had included in its statement of policy the following language which is still in the statute:

Sec. 702 (a). Recognizing . . . (2) that many . . . children have a cultural heritage which differs from that of English-speaking persons; (3) that a primary means by which a child learns is through the use of such child's language and cultural heritage; . . . (5) that . . . children . . . benefit through the fullest utilization of multiple language and cultural resources. . . .

In 1978 even very strong transition program advocates supported the cultural continuance aspect of the program.

MR. HEFTEL (D. Hawaii): The children with the assistance of volunteer instructors within the system develop self-appreciation programs for their own cultures. I have attended their programs and it is apparent this need exists. . . .

MR. McGUIRE: I would agree that the ability to speak, to write English, is very important. I think the key to this is the sensitivity with which we build their English proficiency. The sensitivity issue and the bicultural issue comes [sic] in so that as children come in, it must not be done at the expense of their own culture.[109]

But again there was a modification of the bilingual education law in the 1978 amendments (shown in the italicized portion below) toward integrating and balancing this cultural requirement with the cultural interests of English-speaking students. Bilingual instruction for children of limited English proficiency is to be given "with appreciation for the cultural heritage of such children, *and of other children in American Society. . . .*" (emphasis supplied).[110]

The House of Representatives 1978 Report explained the amendment as follows:

Regarding the question of whether bilingual programs should have a cultural component, the Committee bill amends the present law to require that, if instruction is included on the cultural heritage of the children with limited English language skills, instruction must be also included on the cultural heritage of other children. In addition, the bill requires that research be conducted on the degree to which the inclusion of cultural heritage instruction in a bilingual education program serves to assist children in learning English.[111]

Program Design

The legislation envisions the funds will be used for instruction, teacher training, curriculum development, research, and evaluation.

Instruction

There appears to have been general agreement from the outset on the definition of bilingual education as the use of English and another language as instructional mediums in an educational program. The legislation calls for the "instruction . . . in, and study of, English and, to the extent necessary, to allow a child to achieve competence in the English language, the native language . . . and such instruction [shall be] given with appreciation for the cultural heritage of such children, and of other children in American society. . . ."[112] Bilingual education is to range over the entire curriculum: "to the extent necessary, . . . in all courses or subjects of study which will allow a child to progress effectively through the educational system. . . ."[113]

The 1968 definition of limited English-speaking ability as "children who come from environments where the dominant language is other than English" made no distinction in levels of proficiency nor did it speak to the participation of minority language children in the integrated classroom. In a number of cases, school systems installed bilingual programs and concentrated on teaching English-dominant minority children, placing such children in remedial bilingual programs with minimal use of the non-English language.

Therefore, the present legislation is concerned with integrating the students of limited English proficiency with the rest of the school children both on educational and ethnic grounds. Thus, in "such courses or subjects of study as art, music, and physical education," the statute requires bilingual education programs to provide for participation "in regular classes."[114] The same rationale lies behind the legislative charge that children in bilingual education programs "be placed to the extent practicable, in classes with children of approximately the same age and level of educational attainment."[115] If children of "varying ages or levels of educational attainment are placed in the same class," instruction should be appropriate for their level of attainment.[116] Although teacher training and curriculum development may be centralized, the program shall serve children "in the school which they normally attend."[117]

There was considerable discussion of when and how to include English-speaking students in bilingual education programs. The original 1968 law made no provision for the participation of the English-speaking student in the bilingual program. The 1978 Senate bill allowed the participation of English-speaking children in the bilingual program provided the number did not exceed forty percent. This was a slight reduction from the 50/50 ratio used in Colorado which Congress was advised had worked rather well[118] but still permitted flexibility.[119] The purpose of this provision was to reduce the possibility of segregation in the program and to provide peer models for children with limited English proficiency.

The House bill handled the question somewhat differently, adopting separate rules for programs which remove the children from regular classroom activities, so-called "pull-out" programs. For those programs where the children have the benefit of teaching specialists, only children with limited English proficiency would be eligible. All regular classroom instruction would permit a mix.[120] This approach, perhaps, reflected the GAO criticism: "[T]here often seemed to be too many English-speaking children in the project classrooms, thereby diluting program services for the limited English-speaking children."[121] The final law adopted the Senate language.[122]

The 1975 study conducted by OE's Office of Planning, Budget, and Evaluation identified four exemplary basic classroom bilingual projects that could serve as replicable models for districts contemplating similar programs. The descriptions of these programs were packaged and distributed to interested applicants as Project Information Packages.[123] They were also described to the Congress by the administration, without, however, any suggestion that these would be the only models utilized or even the preferred ones. The structure of the models varies; for example, one project uses English primarily, with one-third of the day in French, while another begins primarily in Spanish and introduces English as the student demonstrates readiness and understanding. In 1978 the Congress required the development of other models as well.

Training

From the outset the need was recognized for specialized training to create the teaching corps and ancillary personnel to serve the program. Thus, the 1968 Bilingual Education Act provided for "pre-service training, designed to prepare persons to participate in bilingual education."[124] The GAO and the American Institutes for Research in their evaluations, the administration in its presentation, and Congress after reviewing the program have all agreed on the need for additional qualified teachers.[125] The issue is one of both quality and quantity.

The 1974 amendments expanded the training component of the existing legislation requiring a fifteen percent set-aside of local bilingual education funding for inservice training.[126] The 1978 legislation removed the fifteen percent inservice training requirement[127] of the statute.

Regarding in-service training, the mandatory 15% set-aside for that purpose is very crucial for some local programs. For others, the need may have been fulfilled and therefore the funds may be better used for other purposes. The Committee bill, therefore, removes the requirements in present law that each local project must expend at least 15% of its funds on in-service teacher training. Rather, the decision on the exact degree of such funding would be left with the local school district, with the expectation that in-service training is an important component of these programs. However, it must be noted that this set-aside funds in-service training programs that are non-degree in nature and therefore may not completely solve the need for highly qualified teachers.[128]

The commissioner may provide a wide range of training through grants, contracts, and fellowships (including stipends and allowances for dependents) to meet specific needs and to promote general career development.[129] The training may be given to teachers, administrators, counselors, paraprofessionals, teacher aides, and parents.[130] Fellowship assistance must be repaid by the trainee either in cash or by an equivalent period of work in bilingual education training. The commission may waive repayment "in extraordinary circumstances."[131]

HEW requires grantees to give priority to persons who are bilingual and who demonstrate a high degree of interest in bilingual education.[132] A grantee which provides training leading to an undergraduate degree or a teaching certificate or training of personnel at an institute of higher education "shall require that all participants in its training program demonstrate proficiency in English and in the target language as a condition of successful completion of the program.[133]

Training may be conducted by: (1) local educational agencies, (2) state educational agencies, and (3) institutions of higher education (including junior colleges and community colleges). Private nonprofit organizations may also provide training if they apply after consultation with, or jointly with, local educational agencies or the state education agency.[134] (The requirement of consultation may be contrasted with the program grant requirements in which a joint application with the local education agency is required.) The commissioner must give priority to applicants with "demonstrated competence and experience in the field of bilingual education."[135]

Curriculum Development

As the federal bilingual education program has expanded (there are now over 70 languages serving 302,000 children) the need for materials has expanded also. The program has not been able to meet this need especially in the less frequently used languages in the United States.

A recent study of the state of bilingual materials, published after the 1978 legislation had passed Congress, reaffirmed this shortage.[136] The study was optimistic in believing that "with growing numbers of bilingual programs and students, bilingual materials development in the U.S. will increase in the years ahead, particularly for the major languages."[137]

In 1975 the Office of Bilingual Education began to fund a network of institutions (materials development centers, dissemination and assessment centers, and training resource centers) pursuant to the statutory mandate that the commissioner and the directors of the National Institute of Education "shall, through competitive contracts with appropriate public agencies and private institutions and organizations, develop and disseminate instructional materials and equipment suitable for bilingual education programs."[138] At present there are thirty-three centers serving more than 500 local education agencies in thirty-nine states, the District of Columbia, Puerto Rico, and the territories of the United States. Each center has specific territorial and linguistic responsibilities.

This program has had considerable impact but the continuing shortages in some areas and weakness in others led to the 1978 amendment requiring the bilingual materials to be equal in quality to those developed for regular English instruction.[139]

> Despite the progress of the materials development centers, a need still exists for high quality materials, especially in some of the Native American, Asian and Pacific, and Indo-European languages. Some Native American projects experience particular problems with languages that do not have a written orthography; local teachers and directors must spend considerable time developing materials in these instances, a task for which few have adequate training.
>
> Existing materials are often unsatisfactory. The GAO report found that 60 percent of project directors and teachers surveyed felt their materials were inadequate. Much of the material sent to the dissemination centers is found to be unsuitable. One dissemination center director estimated that only 10 to 15% of materials received is suitable for dissemination.[140]

The availability of materials already in existence must be considered, and "special attention shall be given to language groups for whom private organizations are unlikely to develop such materials."[141]

Research   The failure to prove the effectiveness of bilingual education and the devastating evaluations by GAO and the American Institutes of Research disturbed the Congress, and it responded by increasing the amount available for research[142] fourfold to $20 million for 1979.[143]

The House Committee Report commented:

> Based on the lack of national data regarding other types of Title VII programs, the lack of national evaluations of other approaches to English instruction, the evidence of gains in individual projects, and the support for the bilingual approach from involved teachers and students and language group organizations, the Committee feels the need for program change as well as for further research, demonstration and evaluation to determine what constitutes a good program of bilingual education.
>
> The Commissioner's Report on the Condition of Bilingual Education of 1977 found that "there is little to guide educators in designing and implementing effective bilingual projects." The National Association for Bilingual Education testified that only a small number of program models have been identified to date.
>
> Consequently, the Committee bill increases the authorization of appropriations for research and development in bilingual education from $5 million a year to $20 million a year.[144]

The commissioner is charged to carry out a research program through competitive contracts with institutions of higher education, private and nonprofit organizations, state educational agencies, and individuals.

The research activities to be funded are set forth in the statute and are wide-ranging. Almost all arose in 1978 at Senate initiative:

1. Studies to determine and evaluate effective models for bilingual bicultural programs;

2. studies to determine
    a. language acquisition characteristics and
    b. the most effective method of teaching English within the context of a bilingual bicultural program;

3. a five-year longitudinal study to measure the effect of bilingual education on students who have non-English language proficiencies;

4. studies to identify the most effective and reliable method of identifying students entitled to bilingual education services;

5. the operation of a clearinghouse of information for bilingual education;

6. studies to determine the most effective methods of teaching reading to children and adults who have language proficiencies other than English;

7. studies to determine the effectiveness of teacher training preservice and inservice programs funded under this title;

8. studies to determine the critical cultural characteristics of selected groups of individuals in order to teach about culture in the program.[145]

Evaluation

Like research, evaluation gained strong support from the Congress in the 1978 legislation primarily because of the GAO report.

The House Committee commented:

> At the local level, a GAO report on bilingual education noted that evaluations for individual projects "have been inadequate for measuring programs' effect on student achievement and . . . have been inadequate for identifying projects worthy of replication." Poor self-evaluation designs proliferated even among the best projects, GAO continued.[146]

The need for local evaluation is also noted in the Senate Report.

> The bill also requires that the Commissioner develop guidelines for local evaluations. It is hoped that these guidelines will provide scientifically valid information as well as describe the unique features of each project in order that local level projects can be validly compared.[147]

The statute also provides that any child enrolled more than two years in the program shall have an individual evaluation.[148] Although designed primarily to transfer responsibility of the program to the states, the provision also assures additional educational data.

The Allocation Process

Although the bilingual education program is a discretionary grant program, the legislation itself and the legislative history impose a structure on the allocation of funds. From the outset, in 1968, there were three general standards imposed:

1. The geographic distribution of children of limited English proficiency in the nation;

2. the capability of local educational agencies to carry out the programs; and

3. the relative number of persons from low-income families to be benefited by such programs.[149]

Geographic Distribution

The requirement to consider the location of children of limited English proficiency in the distribution of bilingual education funds parallels the approach of formula grant programs. The Office of Education has not published data or statistics setting forth the placement of numbers of students with limited English proficiency. The National Center for Education Statistics has tabulated and displayed states with children 4-13 years old with a household language other than English.[150]

There are two other geographical requirements which are to receive priority treatment by the commissioner:

1. Areas having the greatest need for programs;[151] and

2. applications from local educational agencies which are located in various geographical regions of the nation and which propose to assist children of limited English proficiency who have historically been underserved by programs of bilingual education.[152]

The 1978 House Report elaborated on the first standard:

> "Areas of greatest need" should be defined as including those which, within the immediately five preceding years, have had a significantly above-average influx of individuals of limited English language skills.[153]

The second "priority" is weakened considerably by the statutory condition "taking into consideration the relative numbers of such children in the schools for such local educational agencies and the relative need of such programs."[154] Its basic purpose was, given the limited amount of bilingual education funds, "to utilize scarce funds for demonstration programs and projects with a view toward stimulating interest and initiatives among State and local educational agencies throughout the Nation which ultimately would lead to successful non-Federal programs."[155]

Local Education Agency Capability

The regulations setting forth criteria for evaluating individual applications require the application to discuss methods of administration, financial management procedures, coordination of funded and nonfunded activities under the program, and a plan for continuing the program after federal funding is completed.[156]

The 1978 amendments require the commissioner to determine that the assistance

> will contribute toward building the capacity of the applicant to provide a program of bilingual education on a regular basis . . . of sufficient size, scope, and quality to promise significant improvement in the education of children of limited English proficiency and that the applicant will have the resources and commitment to continue the program when assistance under the Title is reduced or no longer available.[157]

Low Income

The low-income criterion originated in the 1968 Senate bill which had required the commissioner to allot funds based on the number of Spanish-speaking students in the states and the per capita income of the states "in such manner as he determines will best carry out the purpose of this title."[158]

The 1968 House bills focused more closely on the low-income question, perhaps reinforced by the experiences of Head Start and other poverty programs which had experimented with bilingual education. Thus, one House bill spoke of projects providing "reasonable assurances of making a substantive impact in meeting the special educational needs of persons who come from non-English-speaking low-income families."[159] Another required the commissioner to "develop criteria and procedures to assure that funds will go to areas of greatest needs," taking into consideration the number of children from non-English-speaking backgrounds and the per capita income from each state.[160]

The 1968 act was a compromise granting the commissioner some discretion while at the same time emphasizing the poverty criteria both in the geographical distribution of the program and in funding specific applications. The commissioner was charged with giving "highest priority to States and areas within States having the greatest need for programs . . . taking into consideration the number of children with limited English speaking ability between the ages of three and eighteen within each State,"[161] and approving those applications "designed to meet the special educational needs of children of limited English speaking abilities in schools having a high concentration of such children from families (a) with income below $3,000 per year, or (b) [receiving payments from State-approved AFDC programs]."[162]

The present law as a result of the 1974 amendments softens somewhat the low-income requirements. It mandates the commissioner *"to the extent feasible* [to] allocate funds appropriated in proportion to the geographical distribution of children of limited English proficiency throughout the Nation with due regard for the relative ability of particular local educational agencies to carry out such programs and the *relative numbers of persons from low-income families sought to be benefited by such programs* (emphasis supplied)."[163]

Low income is defined in the regulations issued by the Office of Education as an annual family income that does not exceed the poverty level determined under Section 111(c)(2) of Title I of the Elementary and Secondary Education Act of 1965 as amended.[164]

The Application Process for Program Grants

Eligibility

To receive bilingual education program grants, one or more local educational agencies or an institution of higher education (including junior and community colleges), in conjunction with one or more local educational agencies, may apply.

State education agencies may apply for funds to provide technical assistance and coordination of bilingual programs within the state. These funds must supplement not supplant other funds available to the state.[165] The state agency may only receive up to five percent of the total that school districts in that state receive for the program.[166] This statutory limitation has caused administrative difficulties in some of the states with smaller bilingual education programs.[167]

Content of Grant Applications

Each grant application must set forth a description of the activities to be funded and provide evidence that the activities "will make substantial progress toward making programs of bilingual education available to children having need thereof in the area served by the applicant."[168]

By regulation, the commissioner has requested evidence assuring applicant supervision and information on the method of administration.[169] Similarly the applicant must set forth the description of fiscal control and the budget justification.

The applicant must indicate (a) the total number and percentage of children of limited English-speaking ability enrolled in the schools of the applicant and the number and percentage to be served by the proposed program; (b) when and how the applicant identified the children; (c) the number of low-income persons sought to be benefited and how they will benefit; (d) provisions for involving qualified personnel with experience in the educational problems of children of limited English-speaking ability and the use of cultural and educational resources in the area to be served; and (e) the evaluation design of the proposed program including, provisions for comparing performance of participating children on tests of reading skills in English and the other language with an estimate of performance in the absence of the program or with nonparticipating children;[170] the instruments of measurement; and provisions for reporting pretest and posttest scores.[171]

The 1978 amendments provide for increased parental participation. An application for a program of bilingual education shall be developed in consultation with an advisory council, a majority of which shall be parents and other representatives of children of limited English proficiency. The application must contain documentation of the advisory council's consultation and comments on the project.[172]

Finally, the application must assure that, after approval, the applicant will provide for continuing consultation and participation by a committee of parents, teachers, and other interested individuals. It would appear that the postapproval consultative group need not be the same as the advisory council. On the committee parents of children participating in the program must predominate, and a majority must be parents of children with limited English proficiency.[173] All parents of participating children must be informed of the institutional goals of the program and the progress of their children.[174]

Duration

In 1978, as in 1974, the duration of project funding was an issue discussed at some length by both the administration and Congress. The Carter administration proposed a five year funding limitation, a position which was supported by the House bill.

> The Committee bill proposes a general rule that assistance under the Act be limited to no more than 5 years for any particular school or group of schools. However, a waiver of this rule is mandated whenever the school district shows a clear fiscal inability to carry on the program; shows adequate progress in the program; and either has a continuing presence of a substantial number of students with limited English-speaking skills in such school or schools, has experienced a recent substantial increase in the number of such students, or is under an obligation to provide bilingual education pursuant to a court order or a Title VI plan.[175]

The Senate opposed such a limitation; although it recognized that state and local commitment is important for the success of the program, the educational needs of the children, in their view, predominated.

> Many local districts are hard pressed for funds at present, and bilingual education for minority students may be a low priority. Without federal funding many children will not receive the help they need. There is no educational base for such a limitation. In most areas with high concentrations of children with limited English proficiency, there are children continually entering the school system—some because of local births and some because of migration. The presence of children needing bilingual education will not disappear after five years. The Committee also noted that no other program in ESEA has such a limitation.[176]

The issue of duration reflected more than budgetary concerns. A firm time limit in Title VII program grants was consistent with a limited federal commitment to bilingual education as a research and development program and a transitional program[177]; open-ended grants suggested a broader federal involvement, a service program, and a maintenance effort.[178]

The 1978 law permits initial funding of one to three years and limits the ability of the commissioner to terminate the program. The commissioner's decision regarding the length of initial funding depends upon (a) the severity of the problem to be addressed, (b) the nature of the activities proposed, (c) the likely duration of the problems addressed by the application, and (d) other criteria the commissioner may establish to assure the effective use of the funds.[179] In addition the commissioner must determine that federal assistance will contribute toward building local capacity to provide a self-sustaining bilingual education program.[180]

Termination provisions are very formal. The commissioner, after reviewing program operations, may, upon finding that a school does not have a long-term need for continued assistance, issue an order to the local educational agency to prepare and submit within one year a revised application setting forth a schedule for termination of federal funding "in the fifth year following the issuance of such an order."[181] The commissioner's finding may not be issued without notice and opportunity for hearing. The reduction schedule shall be in accordance with criteria established by the commissioner designed to ensure gradual assumption of the cost by the applicant.[182]

The commissioner may not issue an "order to submit an application in preparation for termination of assistance . . . to any local educational agency" which shows adequate progress in meeting the goals of the program and a "fiscal inability" to carry on a program without the federal assistance. Further, to prevent termination there must also be either a continuing presence of a substantial number of students of limited English proficiency in bilingual education programs under Title VII; a recent, substantial increase in the number of students of limited English proficiency who have enrolled in such a program; or a state or federal court order or plan approved by the secretary under Title VI of the Civil Rights Act of 1964 affecting services for more children.[183] Once a termination order is issued, the commissioner is further charged to annually review the conditions to see if the order should be withdrawn or suspended.[184]

Program Administration

The law establishes an Office of Bilingual Education run by a director "to whom the Commissioner shall delegate all of his delegable functions relating to bilingual education." Under the 1978 amendments "the director shall also be assigned responsibility for coordinating the bilingual education aspects of other programs administered by the Commissioner."[185]

The statute requires the secretary to establish a National Advisory Council on Bilingual Education composed of fifteen members.[186] At least eight shall be persons experienced in "dealing with the educational problems of children and other persons who are of limited English proficiency." At least one of these eight shall represent persons serving on boards of education operating bilingual education. The group shall consist of at least two experienced teacher trainers, two persons with general experience in elementary and secondary education, two classroom teachers who have utilized bilingual methods and techniques, two parents of students whose language is other than English, one representative of a state educational agency, and one at-large member.

The council shall generally represent the geographical areas and population of persons with limited English proficiency. The secretary shall designate the chairperson and provide staff assistance and information necessary to the council's activities.

The council's function is to advise the commissioner in the preparation of general regulations and administrative and operational policy matters including approval criteria for applications. Each year by March 31, the council shall submit a report to the Congress and the president on the condition of bilingual education in the nation and on the administration and operations of Title VII.

Future Directions

The bilingual education program as originally formulated, and as presently authorized, is a research and demonstration program. Congress acted on an intuitive judgment that teaching children in the language they understand was likely to be helpful. Testimony in 1967 had focused on need with a conscious awareness that solutions as yet were uncertain. The declaration of policy in the 1968 act articulated this perception by looking to local educational agencies "to develop and carry out new and imaginative elementary and secondary school programs."[187]

This language was reinforced in subsequent sections of the act which spoke of "the development of programs . . . including research projects, *pilot* projects . . . designed to *test the effectiveness. . . .*" (emphasis supplied). Congress, in addition, envisioned "the development and dissemination of special instructional materials."[188] In subsequent years as the program has expanded, this initial experimental thrust has become diluted, and the program has moved toward a service emphasis.

Both the 1978 law and congressional reports emphasized once more the research and demonstration character of the program, stressing the need for additional study and evaluation of the approaches. The 1978 amendments specifically added in the statement of policy a subsection to note this direction: "Recognizing . . . (7) research and evaluation capabilities in the field of bilingual education need to be strengthened."

Service Rather Than Demonstration

The Committee bill . . . provides increased authorizations for training activities, research and evaluation and grants. . . . The committee is pleased to note that its faith in the efficacy of bilingual education is being affirmed in a growing number of States which have adopted sound bilingual programs to meet specific needs. It may be that a more direct Federal contribution to such State and local activities is appropriate for the future; but little progress toward such a service orientation can be made until Federal officials charged with carrying out the Title VII program do the job so clearly theirs under the law.[189]

The reaffirmation of the demonstration nature of the program resulted from two congressional concerns: (1) the absence of documentation and statistics which had been requested in 1974 and (2) the damaging reports of GAO[190] and the American Institutes for Research.[191] The AIR study concluded that "there is no compelling evidence in the current data of the Impact Study that Title VII bilingual education as presently implemented is the most appropriate approach for these students." This latter, most recent evaluation troubled the Congress and, although challenged by NIE and others, affected the 1978 legislation, reinforcing the committee's feeling that the appropriate approach and utility of bilingual education needed to be demonstrated.

The first national evaluation of bilingual education supported by the Office of Education and conducted by the American Institutes for Research raises some serious questions about the viability of the bilingual approach.

A recent GAO report on bilingual education pointed out that evaluations for individual projects "have been inadequate for measuring programs' effect on student achievement and . . . have been inadequate for identifying projects worthy of replication."

Consequently, the Committee bill increases the authorization of appropriations for research and development on bilingual education from $5 million a year to $20 million a year. The bill also requires each local project to provide for its own evaluation. It is hoped that these amendments will all lead to greater knowledge within the next several years about what is most effective in bilingual education.[192]

To assure that additional data is available and that there is an understanding in the Congress of the overall direction of the program, the 1978 amendments require the individual grant applications to include an evaluation component.[193] In addition, the Commissioner of Education is required to report annually to the Congress. The 1978 law reiterates the 1974 requirements with minor modifications. The commissioner, in consultation with the National Advisory Council, shall submit:

1. A national assessment of the educational needs of children and other persons with limited English proficiency

2. A report on the degree to which these needs are being met by federal, state, and local efforts

3. A plan, including cost estimates, for extending bilingual education to serve preschool and elementary children and other persons of limited English proficiency, including a phased plan for training of necessary teachers and other educational personnel

4. An evaluation of the bilingual program

5. A description of the staffing of the program by HEW

6. An assessment of the number of teachers and other personnel needed to carry out a program of bilingual education for persons of limited English proficiency

7. An estimate of the number of teacher training fellowships for bilingual education which will be necessary for the two succeeding fiscal years[194]

Most importantly, the secretary is charged with additional actions and reports which elaborate upon these requirements. By September 30, 1980, the secretary is to develop (a) methods to identify children of limited English proficiency who are in need of bilingual education programs; (b) "evaluation and data gathering models, which take into account linguistic and cultural differences of the child, which consider the availability and the operations of State programs for such children, and shall include allowances for variables which are applicable" to bilingual education programs "such as pupil-teacher ratios, teacher qualifications, length of the program, hours of instruction, percentage of children in the classroom who are English dominant and the percentage who have limited English proficiency."[195]

As part of this developmental effort, the commissioner was to publish within six months of the date of passage of the Education Amendments of 1978 "(1) models for programs of bilingual education which may include suggested teacher-pupil ratios, teacher qualifications, and other factors affecting the quality of instruction offered, and which shall represent a variety of types of such programs, and (2) models for the evaluation of such programs as to the progress made by participants therein attaining English skills."[196] The House of Representatives reported the following explanation of this mandate:

> The Commissioner's Report on the Condition of Bilingual Education of 1977 found that "there is little to guide educators in designing and implementing effective bilingual projects." The National Association for Bilingual Education testified that only a small number of program models have been identified to date.[197]

Although the committee's reports reflected the skepticism and concern with the evaluations to date, the lack of data on student needs and teacher availability, and the absence of clear instruction models, the act looked toward developing a service program on a broad level throughout the United States, once models had been developed and proved. The steady increase in appropriations from $7.5 million in fiscal year 1969 to $158.6 million in fiscal year 1979,[198] indicates both a desire and possible capacity to effect such a conversion. Such a modification envisions changing, as well, the method of distributing funds from a discretionary grant program to formula distribution.

> (f) The Secretary shall prepare and submit to the President and to the Congress not later than December 31, 1981, a report setting forth recommendations on the methods of converting, not later than July 1, 1984, the bilingual education program from a discretionary grant program to a formula grant program to serve students of limited English proficiency and recommendations on whether or not such conversion would best serve the needs of such students. The study required by this subsection shall consider the findings of other studies required to be made under this section, and shall include cost estimates for the phasing in of the formula grant program.[199]

The discussion to convert from a research and demonstration program to a service program is likely to center not only on measurable success but also on cost. The general charge to utilize funds to initiate bilingual programs has continued, but the 1978 House Report specifically noted the cost question in its lengthy discussion of demonstration v. service. It hoped that once a program was established, costs would decrease and local districts would continue the program.[200] One can conjecture that if the demonstrations prove favorable, if the costs of continuing a program are shown to be substantially less than initiating a program, and if local districts are unable to meet the entire financial burden, Congress will support a bilingual education service program.

Bilingual education programs are funded not only under Title VII but also under a number of other programs in HEW.[201] The increased power granted to the director of the Title VII office over these other programs and the transfer of Section 708(c) of the Emergency School Aid Act to Title VII[202] foreshadow a centralized administration and, perhaps, an overall, cohesive, educational concern with minority language children.

The Emergency School Aid Act bilingual set-aside funds, curriculum development, teacher training, and interethnic understanding programs help provide equal educational opportunity for children with language difficulties. The funds may be utilized to assist school districts to meet *Lau* remedy court orders.

The House Committee commented on the provision: "The Committee was disturbed to find little coordination between this program and Title VII . . . this transfer will achieve a greater coordination between the two programs."[203]

Further evidence of this centralized direction is seen in the new legislation establishing a Department of Education. This legislation establishes an Office of Bilingual Education and Minority Languages Affairs headed by a director who "shall coordinate the administration of bilingual education programs by the Department and shall consult with the Secretary concerning policy decisions affecting bilingual education and minority language affairs."[204] The Senate bill called for an Office of Bilingual Education and Minority Affairs. In adopting the House nomenclature, the final law singled out the problems of language and language minority individuals from persons designated for special treatment by race, color, sex, or income. The role of the director is not confined to bilingual education. He is given a broader consultative role in minority language affairs as well.

The director gains additional stature under the reorganization. He/she reports directly to the secretary[205] and is expected to be established at a GS-18, the top level of the Civil Service. The Senate bill specified a GS-18 rating for the director while the House stated no specific grade level. The grade was omitted in the final law with the comment in the committee report that "the conferees wish to indicate their intentions that this official should be so classified by the Office of Personnel Management."[206]

A Coordinated Bilingual Education Program with Increased Significance

Conclusion

Over the last ten years since the Bilingual Education Act was first passed, Title VII programs have expanded considerably in numbers, and funding has continually increased. As this has occurred, Congress has sought greater formalization of the program, clarification of its goals and direction, and development of standards of success.

It appears likely that the future of the program depends upon establishing clear evaluative criteria and a record of success. The new law seeks local capacity building to assure continuity, but is less clear on the long-range federal commitment.

With the broader stature of the director of bilingual education in the new Department of Education, there is increased opportunity to bring together minority language education programs. One of the major challenges facing the director will be the coordination of the various minority language programs outside of Title VII.

Selected Legislative History Documents

Bilingual Education Act: **1968**
P.L. 90-247, (Jan. 2, 1968), 81 Stat. 816, 20 U.S.C.A.
880 (b)

Rules and Regulations:
39 Fed. Reg. 17963 (May 22, 1974)

Congressional Reports:
U.S. Sen., Committee on Labor and Public Welfare,
Elementary and Secondary Education Act Amendments of
1967, Report No. 90-726 (90th Cong., 1st Sess.)

House of Rep., Committee on Education and Labor,
Elementary and Secondary Education Act Amendments of
1967, Report No. 90-1049 (90th Cong., 1st Sess.)

Congressional Hearings:
U.S. Sen., Bilingual Education, Hearings before the Special Subcommittee on Bilingual Education of the Committee on Labor and Public Welfare on S. 428 (2 vols.) (90th
Cong., 1st Sess.)

House of Rep., Bilingual Education Programs, Hearings
before the General Subcommittee on Education of the
Committee on Education and Labor on H.R. 9840 and
H.R. 10224 (90th Cong., 1st Sess.)

1974

Bilingual Education Act:
P.L. 93-380, (Aug. 21, 1974), 88 Stat. 503

Rules and Regulations:
45 C.F.R. 581, Part 123 Bilingual Education

Congressional Reports:
U.S. Sen., Committee on Labor and Public Welfare, Education Amendments of 1974, Report No. 93-763 (93rd Cong., 2nd Sess.)

House of Rep., Committee on Education and Labor, Education Amendments of 1974, Report No. 93-1211 (93rd Cong., 2nd Sess.)

House of Rep., Committee on Education and Labor, Education Amendments of 1974, Report No. 93-805 (93rd Cong., 2nd Sess.)

Congressional Hearings:
U.S. Sen., Education Legislation, 1973, Hearings before the Subcommittee on Education of the Committee on Labor and Public Welfare on S. 1539 (93rd Cong., 1st Sess.), Part 7

House of Rep., Elementary and Secondary Education Amendments of 1973, Hearings before the General Subcommittee on Education of the Committee on Education and Labor on H.R. 16, H.R. 69, H.R. 5163, and H.R. 5823 (93rd Cong., 1st Sess.)

1978

Bilingual Education Act:
P.L. 95-561, (Nov. 1, 1978), 92 Stat. 2270

Rules and Regulations (Proposed):
44 Fed. Reg. 38415 (June 29, 1979)

Rules and Regulations (Final):
45 Fed. Reg. 23208 (April 4, 1980)

Congressional Reports:
U.S. Sen., Committee on Human Resources, Educational Amendments of 1978, Report No. 95-856 (95th Cong., 2nd Sess.)

House of Rep., Committee on Education and Labor, Education Amendments of 1978, Report No. 95-1137 (95th Cong., 2nd Sess.)

House of Rep., Committee on Education and Labor, Education Amendments of 1978, Report No. 95-1753 (95th Cong., 2nd Sess.) (Conference Report)

Congressional Hearings:
U.S. Sen., Education Amendments of 1978, Hearings before the Subcommittee on Education of the Committee on Human Resources on S. 1753 (95th Cong., 1st Sess.)

House of Rep., Bilingual Education, Hearings before the Subcommittee on Elementary, Secondary, and Vocational Education of the Committee on Education and Labor on H.R. 15 (95th Cong., 1st Sess.)

NOTES

1. To a degree, of course, there is some implicit recognition of English since the Constitution is written in that language.

2. See generally, E. McWhinney, *Federal Constitution-Making for a Multi-National World* (1966); R. Bowie and C. Friedrich, *Studies in Federalism* (1954). The bilingual experience of Canada is detailed in Royal Commission on Biculturalism and Bilingualism, *A Preliminary Report* 33 (1965).

3. R. Fitzgibbon, *The Constitutions of the Americas* 228, 323, 398, 448, 556, 605 (1948) cites the following constitutions in the Western Hemisphere that designate official languages: Cuba, article 6; Ecuador, article 7; Guatemala, article 4; Haiti, article 29; Nicaragua, article 7; and Panama, article 7.

4. *The Federalist Papers,* No. II (1788).

5. H. Manuel, *Spanish-Speaking Children of the Southwest* (1956).

6. T. Fehrenbach, *Lone Star: A History of Texas and the Texans* 167 (1968).

7. D. Ferris, *Judge Marvin and the Founding of the California Public School System* 92 (1962).

8. Calif. Stat. Ch. 556, Sec. 55 (1870).

9. L. Pitt, *The Decline of the Californios* 226 (1966).

10. In 1884 the law required "Each of the voting precincts of a county shall be and constitute a school district in which shall be . . . taught reading, writing . . . in either English or Spanish or both, as the directors may determine." H. Kloss, *The American Bilingual Tradition* 134 (1977).

11. J. Forbes, "Mexican-Americans: A Handbook for Educators," in *Hearings before the House General Subcommittee on Education of the Committee on Education and Labor on H.R. 9840 and H. 10224*, 90th Cong., 1st Sess., 508 (1967).

12. Kloss 134-135 (1977).

13. N. Gonzales, "The Spanish Americans of New Mexico: A Distinctive Heritage" in University of California, *Mexican-American Study Project* 36-38 (1967); W. Keleher, *The Fabulous Frontier* 90 (1945).

14. F. Cohen, *Handbook of Federal Indian Law* 234 (1942).

15. Ibid., 240.

16. One treaty did, however, include a reference to the language to be employed. This notable exception appears in the Treaty of May 6, 1828, with the Cherokee Nation. Article 5 reads in part: "It is further agreed by the U.S. to pay $1,000 . . . towards the purchase of a Printing Press and Types to aid towards the Cherokees in the progress of education, and to benefit and enlighten them as people, *in their own language*" (emphasis supplied).

17. *The Education of American Indians, A Survey of the Literature,* prepared for the Senate Special Subcommittee on Indian Education of the Committee on Labor and Public Welfare, 91st Cong., 1st Sess., 11 (1969).

18. "The Indians being the prior occupants, possess the right of the soil. It cannot be taken from them unless by their consent, or by

rights of conquest in case of a just war. To dispossess them on any other principle would be a great violation of the fundamental laws of nature.'' Statement of Henry Knox quoted in D. McNickle, *The Indian Tribes of the United States: Ethnic and Cultural Survival* 32 (1962). See also *Johnson* v. *MacIntosh* 21 U.S. (8 Wheat.) 543 (1823); *Cherokee Nation* v. *Georgia* 30 U.S. (5 Pet.) 1 (1831); and *Worchester* v. *Georgia* 31 U.S. (6 Pet.) 515 (1832).

19. Quoted in Senate Special Subcommittee on Indian Education of the Committee on Labor and Public Welfare, *Indian Education: A National Tragedy—A National Challenge,* 91st Cong., 1st Sess., 143 (1969) (hereinafter cited as *Indian Education).*

20. The Dawes Severalty Act, which ushered in the allotment period of Indian history, was passed in 1884. Its essential features were: (1) tribal lands were to be divided and the president was authorized to assign or allot 160 acres to each Indian family head; (2) each Indian would make his selection, but if he failed or refused, a government agent would make the selection; (3) title to the land was placed in trust for twenty-five years; (4) citizenship was conferred upon all allottees and upon other Indians who abandoned their tribes and adopted ''the habits of civilized life''; (5) surplus tribal lands remaining after allotment might be sold to the United States. McNickle 48-49. The allotment law and subsequent statutes set up procedures which resulted in the transfer of some ninety million acres from Indian to white owners in the next forty-five years. *Indian Education,* pp. 150-151; *Blackfeet et al. Nation* v. *United States,* 81 Ct. Cls. 101, 115, 140 (1935).

21. A. Josephy, Jr., *The Indian Heritage of America* 339 (1947).

22. Superintendent of Indian Schools, *Sixth Annual Report* 10 (1887).

23. A. Faust, *The German Element in the United States* 204 (1969).

24. For example, Missouri in 1817; Illinois in 1825; Michigan in 1835; and Iowa in 1841. H. Kloss, *The Bilingual Tradition in the United States* 200 (1970).

25. Faust 151.

26. Ibid.

27. Ibid., 152.

28. L. Jorgensen, *The Founding of Public Education in Wisconsin* 146 (1956).

29. M. Jones, *American Immigration* 103 (1960).

30. The text has limited itself to immigration from Europe. Similar pressures arose against the Chinese and Japanese migrant in the western states and in Hawaii culminating in a series of laws aimed at restricting immigration, ownership of land, and, subsequently, in pressure to close the private Japanese foreign language schools. See *Farrington* v. *Tokushige* 273 U.S. 284 (1927). See generally M. Konvitz, *The Alien and Asiatic in American Law* (1946) and R. Daniels, *The Politics of Prejudice: The Anti-Japanese Movement in California and the Struggle for Japanese Exclusion* (1969).

31. D. Eaton, *The Government of Municipalities* 123-126 (1899).

32. The detailing of these political and economic requirements and their original purpose is set forth in A. Leibowitz, ''English

Literacy: Legal Sanction for Discrimination," 45 *Notre Dame Lawyer* 7 (1969).

33. A. Leibowitz, *Educational Policy and Political Acceptance: The Imposition of English as the Language of Instruction in American Schools* (1971).

34. *Myers* v. *Nebraska* 262 U.S. 390 (1923).

35. *Lassiter* v. *Northhampton Election Board* 360 U.S. 45 (1959); but see *Cardona* v. *Power* 384 U.S. 672 (1966) and *Puerto Rican Organization for Political Action* v. *Kusper* 490 F. 2nd 575 (7th Cir. 1975).

36. Economic Opportunity Act of 1964. P.L. 88-452, 78 Stat. 508.

37. Elementary and Secondary Education Act of 1965. P.L. 89-10, 79 Stat. 27.

38. The 1930 Census identified "Mexicans" (persons of Spanish colonial descent) as a racial classification. In 1940, on the basis of a five percent sample, the Census counted persons speaking Spanish as the mother tongue. The 1950 and 1960 Censuses, on the basis of a twenty and twenty-five percent sample, respectively, identified the Spanish-surnamed populace in the five southwestern states. These states had accounted for more than eighty percent of all persons with Spanish as the mother tongue. The 1970 Census used four different means of identifying persons of Spanish ancestry: (1) birthplace, (2) Spanish surname, (3) mother tongue, and (4) Spanish origin based on self-identification.

39. The precise figures of 1960 for these three states are: Arizona—194,356 Spanish-surnamed, out of a total population of 1,302,161; New Mexico—269,122 out of a total population of 951,023; and Colorado—157,173 out of a total population of 1,753,050.

40. Hearings before the Senate Special Subcommittee on Bilingual Education of the Committee on Labor and Public Welfare, 90th Cong., 1st Sess., 75 (1967) (hereinafter cited as 1967 Senate Hearings, Bilingual Education).

41. The Nixon administration expanded its jurisdiction and renamed it the Cabinet Committee on Opportunity for the Spanish-Speaking.

42. Upheld by the Supreme Court in *South Carolina* v. *Katzenbach* 383 U.S. 301 (1966). In extending the Voting Rights Act in 1970 and 1975, Congress suspended and then banned the English literacy test.

43. The provision was upheld by the Supreme Court in *Katzenbach* v. *Morgan* 384 U.S. 641 (1966) reversing 247 F. Supp. 196 (DDC 1965).

44. New York City Board of Education, *Puerto Rican Study 1953-1957* (1958).

45. Colorado Commission on Spanish Citizens, *The Status of Spanish-Surnamed Citizens in Colorado* (1967).

46. For example, H.R., Con. Res. 108 (83rd Cong., 1st Sess.).

47. Bilingualism in education, off-reservation boarding schools, and termination were not necessarily at odds although in practice they were seen that way. The most notable experiment in bilingual

education in an off-reservation boarding school (which in practice was linked to relocation) was the special Navajo education program which began in 1946 at the Sherman Institute in Riverside, California, L. Coombs, *Doorway toward the Light* (1962).

48. Senate Special Subcommittee on Indian Education of the Committee on Labor and Public Welfare, *Indian Education: A National Tragedy—A National Challenge,* 91st Cong., 1st Sess., 19 (1969). The point in the text is well taken. However, it should be noted that the Cherokees were far from typical. They were the only North American tribe which had developed an indigenous written language.

49. H.R., Doc. 272 (90th Cong., 2nd Sess.), 5. President Johnson's message on Indian affairs, the most liberal statement of Indian policy ever made, although it stressed Indian education and its control by Indians, did not mention the subject of language. Message from the President of the United States transmitting Indian Policy. H.R. Doc. No. 91-363 (91st Cong., 2nd Sess.).

50. Statement of Dr. Joshua Fishman, Research Professor of Social Sciences, Yeshiva University, 1967 Senate Hearings, Bilingual Education, pp. 133-134.

51. See the testimony of various officials in 1967 Senate Hearings, Bilingual Education; and House of Representatives, Bilingual Education Programs, Hearings before the General Subcommittee on Education of the Committee on Education and Labor, 90th Cong., 1st Sess. (1967) (hereinafter cited as 1967 House Hearings, Bilingual Programs).

52. The literature is vast and rarely are distinctions made between bilingual and other language programs. Good reviews of the literature only slightly dated are P. Engle, *The Use of the Vernacular Languages in Education Revisited: A Literature Review prepared for the Ford Foundation, Office of Mexico, Central American and the Caribbean* (1973); J. Rubin and B. Jernudd, *References for Students of Language Planning* (1974). See also the listing Office of Education, *Publications on Comparative Education* (March 1, 1975). For more substantive material see the papers from the Section on Language Planning submitted to the VIII World Congress of Sociology (Toronto, 1974); the International Conference on Language Planning (Skokloster, Sweden, 1973); and J. Fishman, ed., *Readings in the Sociology of Language* (1965).

53. House Report 95-1137, Education Amendments of 1978 (95th Cong., 2nd Sess.) 84 (hereinafter cited as 1978 House Report).

54. S. 428 (90th Cong, 1st Sess., 1967), §702.

55. Statement of Senator Yarborough, 1967 Senate Hearings, Bilingual Education, p. 37.

56. S. 428 (90th Cong., 1st Sess., 1967), §703(b).

57. Statement of Schmuel Lapin, General Secretary, YIVO Institute of Jewish Research, 1967 Senate Hearings, Bilingual Education, p. 602.

58. Statement of Honorable Henry B. González (Democrat, Texas), 1967 Senate Hearings, Bilingual Education, p. 600.

59. 1967 House Hearings, Bilingual Programs.

60. 20 U.S.C. 880(b) (1968), P.L. 90-247, Title VII, §702, 81 Stat. 816.

61. 1967 Senate Hearings, Bilingual Education, pp. 33-34.

62. Bilingual Education Act as amended, §703(a)(1).

63. Senate Report 95-856, Education Amendments of 1978 (95th Cong., 2nd Sess.) 69 (hereinafter cited as 1978 Senate Report).

64. House of Representatives, Bilingual Education, Hearings before the Subcommittee on Elementary, Secondary, and Vocational Education of the Committee on Education and Labor, 95th Cong., 1st Sess., Part 3, 306-308 (1977) (hereinafter cited as 1977 House Hearings, Bilingual Education).

65. Ibid., 332-333.

66. 1978 House Report, p. 87.

67. P.L. 95-561 (95th Cong., 2nd Sess.), Education Amendments of 1978, 92 Stat. 2143 (hereinafter "Bilingual Education Act as amended"), §703(a)(1).

68. 1978 Senate Report, p. 70.

69. Ibid. The regulations judge groups of children to be "historically underserved" by "comparing the number and distribution, by language group, of children of limited English proficiency who are in need of bilingual education with the number and distribution, by language group, of children of limited English proficiency who are being served by programs of bilingual education." 45 CFR 123a.30.

70. Statement of Bruce Gaarder, Chief, Modern Language Section, U.S. Office of Education, 1967 House Hearings, Bilingual Programs, pp. 351-357.

71. Ibid., 399.

72. Bilingual Education Act of 1968, §706(a). The section referred to in this footnote is as a result of a 1970 amendment, P.L. 91-230, April 13, 1970; 84 Stat. 151.

73. Ibid., see §706(b).

74. Bilingual Education Act as amended, §722(b); cf., Bilingual Education Act of 1968, §706(b).

75. 1978 Senate Report, p. 78.

76. Bilingual Education Act as amended, §721(f). See also 45 CFR 123a.21.

77. 1978 House Report, p. 86.

78. Bilingual Education Act of 1968, 81 Stat. 816, §702.

79. S. 428, (90th Cong., 1st Sess., 1967).

80. 1967 Senate Hearings, Bilingual Education, p. 410.

81. Statement of Senator Ralph Yarborough, ibid., p. 1.

82. C. Lavatelli, *Piaget's Theory Applied to an Early Childhood Education* 42 (1973).

83. Statement of Leonard Pacheco, Project Director, Project Head Start, Alhambra, California, 1967 Senate Hearings, Bilingual Education, p. 422.

84. Statement of Honorable Ernest D. Debs, Supervisor, Los Angeles County, ibid., p. 432.

85. Statement of Robert S. Randall, Associate Director, Research and Evaluation, Southwest Educational Development Laboratory, Austin, Texas, ibid., p. 608.

86. Statement of Professor Julián Nava, Member-Elect, Los Angeles City Board of Education, ibid., p. 436.

87. Statement of Luis Alvarez, Coordinator, Federated Puerto Rican Parents, ibid., p. 567.

88. Statement of Schmuel Lapin, General Secretary, YIVO Institute for Jewish Research, ibid., p. 602.

89. P.L. 90-247, Jan. 2, 1968, Stat. 816, §702.

90. Senate Report 90-726, Elementary and Secondary Education Act Amendments of 1967 (90th Cong., 1st Sess.) 49.

91. Ibid., 50.

92. 1967 House Hearings, Bilingual Programs, pp. 44-45.

93. Senate Report 93-763, Education Amendments of 1974 (93rd Cong., 2nd Sess.) 42 (hereinafter cited as 1974 Senate Report).

94. Quoted in T. Andersson, "Bilingual Educaion: The American Experience," paper presented at the Ontario Institute for Studies in Education Conference on Bilingual Education, Toronto, Canada, March 13, 1971, p. 14, ED 048 581.

95. 1974 Senate Report, p. 45.

96. Bilingual Education Act as amended, §702(a)(7)(B).

97. Ibid., §731(c)(3).

98. American Institutes for Research, *Evaluation of the Impact of ESEA Title VII, Spanish/English Bilingual Education Program: Overview of Study and Findings* 14, 10-11 (1978).

99. Statement of Gary Orfield, Department of Political Science, University of Illinois at Urbana, 1977 House Hearings, Bilingual Education, pp. 336-337.

100. Statement of María Swanson, President, National Association for Bilingual Education, ibid., p. 333.

101. Bilingual Education Act as amended, §703(a)(4)(B).

102. 1978 Senate Report, p. 71.

103. Bilingual Education Act as amended, §703(a)(4)(A)(i).

104. 1978 House Report, p. 87.

105. Ibid.

106. Comptroller General of the United States, *Bilingual Education: An Unmet Need* 45 (1976).

107. U.S. Civil Rights Commission, *A Better Chance to Learn: Bilingual Bicultural Education* (1975).

108. 1977 House Hearings, Bilingual Education, pp. 306-321.

109. Ibid., 345-346.

110. Bilingual Education Act as amended, §703(a)(4)(A)(i).

111. 1978 House Report 95-1137, p. 87.

112. Bilingual Education Act as amended, §703(a)(4)(A).

113. Ibid.

114. Ibid., §703(a)(4)(C).

115. Ibid., §703(a)(4)(D).

116. Ibid.

117. Ibid., §703(a)(4)(B).

118. 1978 House Report, p. 86.

119. 1978 Senate Report, p. 71.

120. 1978 House Report, p. 303.

121. Comptroller General of the United States, *Bilingual Education: An Unmet Need* (1976).

122. Bilingual Education Act as amended, §703(a)(4)(B).

123. Office of Education, Project Savior; Project Venceremos, Project Nuevos Horizontes, Project Adelante.

124. Bilingual Education Act of 1968, §704(b).

125. Comptroller General of the United States, 14. American Institutes for Research, *Evaluation of the Impact of ESEA Title VII, Spanish/English Bilingual Education Program* (1978). The House of Representatives in its 1978 report estimated a national requirement of 129,000 teachers.

126. Bilingual Education Act of 1974, §721(b)(2)(B).

127. Bilingual Education Act as amended, §721(b)(2)(B).

128. 1978 House Report, p. 89.

129. Bilingual Education Act as amended, §723(a)(1)(2).

130. Some of the needs of bilingual teachers and their specialized training is set forth in H. Casso, *Bilingual/Bicultural Education and Teacher Training* (1976).

131. Bilingual Education Act as amended, §723 (a)(6); cash repayment is envisioned over fifteen years at an interest rate of seven percent per annum, 45 CFR 123h.44.

132. 45 CFR 123h.30.

133. 45 CFR 123e.41.

134. Bilingual Education Act as amended, §723(b).

135. Ibid., §723(a)(4).

136. Development Associates, Inc., *A Study of the State of Bilingual Materials Development and the Transition of Materials to the Classroom* (3 vols.) 6, vol. 1 (1978).

137. Ibid., p. 25.

138. Bilingual Education Act as amended, §742(e).

139. Ibid.

140. 1978 House Report, p. 86.

141. Ibid.

142. 1978 House Report, p. 84. Although not official, perhaps equally influential was the critical review—N. Epstein, *Language Ethnicity and the Schools: Policy Alternatives for Bilingual Bicultural Education* (1977).

143. Bilingual Education Act as amended, §742.

144. 1978 House Report, p. 85.

145. Bilingual Education Act as amended, §742(b).

146. 1978 House Report, p. 85.

147. 1978 Senate Report, p. 69.

148. Bilingual Education Act as amended, §721(b)(3)(F).

149. Bilingual Education Act as amended, §721(b)(4); Bilingual Education Act of 1968, §705(b)(2). See also Bilingual Education Act as amended §721(b)(3)(A).

150. National Center for Education Statistics, *The Condition of Education: Statistical Report* 37, Chart 1.15 (1978).

151. Bilingual Education Act as amended, §721(c). The final regulations deemphasized this criterion when comment on the draft regulations regarded it as unfairly discriminating against school districts which were small, rural, or did not have a heavy concentration of children of limited English proficiency. 45 Fed. Reg. 23231 (April 4, 1980).

152. Ibid., §721(b)(4).

153. 1978 House Report, p. 91.

154. Bilingual Education Act as amended, §721(b)(4).

155. 1978 Senate Report, p. 70.

156. 45 CFR 123a.30.

157. Bilingual Education Act as amended, §721(b)(3)(E).

158. S. 428 (90th Cong., 1st Sess., 1967), §703(b).

159. H.R. 9840 (90th Cong., 1st Sess., 1967), §703(b).

160. H.R. 10224 (90th Cong., 1st Sess., 1967), §703(b).

161. Bilingual Education Act of 1968, §703(b).

162. Ibid., §704(a&c).

163. Bilingual Education Act as amended, §721(b)(4) (emphasis supplied).

164. 45 CFR 123.01(e); the allocation formula of Title I is discussed in 1978 House Report, pp. 8-17.

165. Bilingual Education Act as amended, §721(b)(5)(A).

166. Ibid., §721(b)(5)(B).

167. 1977 House Hearings, Bilingual Education, p. 87.

168. Bilingual Education Act as amended, §721(b)(1)(B).

169. 45 CFR 123a.30.

170. Ibid.

171. Ibid.

172. Bilingual Education Act as amended, §703(a)(4)(E).

173. Ibid., §703(a)(4)(E)(iii); 45 CFR 123a.44.

174. Ibid., §703(a)(4)(F).

175. 1978 House Report, p. 88.

176. 1978 Senate Report, p. 71.

177. The time limitation was embodied in the HEW regulation published in October 1973. 45 Fed. Reg. 123 (Oct. 1, 1973).

178. The issue is discussed with respect to the 1974 law in some detail in S. Schneider, *Revolution, Reaction, or Reform: The 1974 Bilingual Education Act* 104 (1976).

179. Bilingual Education Act as amended, §721(e)(1).

180. Ibid., §721(b)(3)(E).

181. Ibid., §721(b)(2)(B).

182. Ibid.

183. Ibid., §721(b)(2)(A)(iii).

184. Ibid., §721(b)(2)(C).

185. Ibid., §731.

186. The role of the Council is set forth ibid., §732.

187. Bilingual Education Act of 1968, §702.

188. Ibid., §704(a).

189. 1978 Senate Report, p. 68. The regulations focus at some length on demonstration projects including additional target populations (children of migratory workers, recent immigrants, high school students preparing to enter the job market, and exceptional children), exemplary approaches to instruction including use of computer assisted instruction, high probability of replication in other similar school districts, and approaches to obtain community/parental involvement. 45 CFR 123b.10, 45 CFR 123b.30.

190. Comptroller General of the United States, *Bilingual Education: An Unmet Need* (1976).

191. American Institutes for Research, *Evaluation of the Impact of ESEA Title VII, Spanish/English Bilingual Education Program* (1978).

192. 1978 House Report, pp. 84-85.

193. Bilingual Education Act as amended, §721(b)(3)(C)(iii).

194. Ibid., §731(c)(1)-(6).

195. Ibid., §731(e).

196. Ibid., §731(d).

197. 1978 House Report, p. 85.

198. "House-Senate Conference Committee Agrees on Bilingual Education Budget," *FORUM* II(8), September 1979, p. 2.

199. Bilingual Education Act as amended, §731(f).

200. 1978 House Report, pp. 87-88.

201. A good listing is found in HEW, *The Condition of Bilingual Education in the Nation: First Report by the U.S. Commissioner of Education to the President and the Congress* (1976).

202. Bilingual Education Act as amended, §751.

203. 1978 House Report, p. 90.

204. House Report 96-459 to accompany S. 210, Department of Education Organization Act (96th Cong., 1st Sess., 1979), p. 9.

205. Ibid., pp. 41-42.

206. Ibid., p. 42.